VIOLIN

TANGO
(Por Una Cabeza)

Solo Violin with Piano Reduction

Lyrics by ALFREDO LE PERA
Music by CARLOS GARDEL

Arranged for Itzhak Perlman
by JOHN WILLIAMS

ISBN 978-1-4234-4225-7

HAL•LEONARD®
CORPORATION
7777 W. BLUEMOUND RD. P.O. BOX 13819 MILWAUKEE, WI 53213

TANGO
(Por Una Cabeza)

Lyrics by ALFREDO Le PERA
Music by CARLOS GARDEL

Arranged for Itzhak Perlman
by JOHN WILLIAMS

VIOLIN

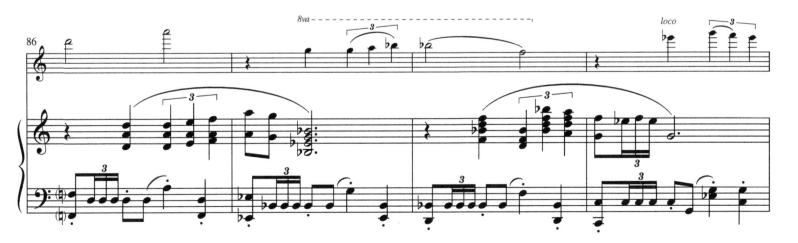

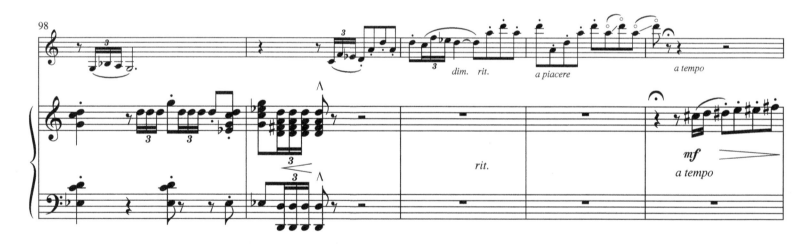